I0409833

Passive Income Power:

Building Financial Freedom through Multiple Streams

Edward Bradley

Building Financial Freedom through Multiple Streams

Passive Income Power

ISBN: 9798851575792

Building Financial Freedom through
Multiple Streams

Passive Income Power

Building Financial Freedom through Multiple Streams

Passive Income Power

Building Financial Freedom through Multiple Streams

Table of Contents

Building Financial Freedom through Multiple
Streams

Passive Income Power

Passive Income Power

Passive Income Power

INTRODUCTION TO PASSIVE INCOME

Welcome to the exciting world of passive income, where your money works for you and opens doors to financial freedom. In this chapter, we will introduce you to the concept of passive income, explain its benefits, and help you understand how it can transform your financial future.

What is Passive Income? Let's start by demystifying passive income. It's money that you earn with minimal effort or ongoing involvement once you set up the income stream. Unlike traditional active income, where you trade your time for money, passive income allows you to make money even while you sleep or enjoy your favorite activities.

The Benefits of Passive Income Passive income offers numerous advantages that can significantly impact your life. We'll explore the benefits, including:

Freedom and flexibility to spend time on what matters most to you.

Reduced reliance on a single income source, providing financial security.

Potential for long-term wealth accumulation and increased financial independence.

How Passive Income Can Change Your Life Passive income has the power to transform your financial future and bring you closer to achieving your dreams. We'll delve into how passive income can:

Help you pay off debts and achieve financial stability.

Create opportunities for early retirement or the pursuit of your passions.

Provide a sense of security and peace of mind for you and your loved ones.

Section 4: Starting Your Passive Income Journey Embarking on a passive income journey requires a mindset shift and a willingness to take action. We'll discuss the importance of setting clear goals, developing a positive attitude, and embracing the learning process. This chapter will lay the foundation for your passive income journey, empowering you to take the first steps towards financial freedom.

 As you conclude this introductory chapter on passive income, you now have a solid understanding of what it means and the potential it holds. You've learned about the benefits of passive income and how it can transform your financial life. Armed with this knowledge, you're ready to embark on your journey towards generating passive income and opening doors to a life of abundance and freedom. Remember, the path to passive income requires dedication, persistence, and a willingness to explore different opportunities. So, let's dive into the exciting world of passive income and start building your wealth one step at a time.

.

THE MINDSET SHIFT FOR PASSIVE INCOME SUCCESS

Welcome to Chapter 2 of our journey towards passive income success. In this chapter, we will explore the importance of cultivating the right mindset for achieving your financial goals. A mindset shift is crucial as you embark on your passive income journey, and it will pave the way for your success.

Embracing the Abundance Mindset To succeed in generating passive income, it's essential to embrace an abundance mindset. This mindset is characterized by a belief that there are limitless opportunities and resources available to you. We'll discuss strategies for shifting from a scarcity mindset, where you focus on limitations and lack, to an abundance mindset, where you see possibilities and abundance all around you.

Overcoming Limiting Beliefs Limiting beliefs can hold you back from achieving your passive income goals. We'll identify common limiting beliefs and provide practical techniques for overcoming them. By challenging and replacing these beliefs with empowering ones, you'll unlock your full potential and open yourself up to new possibilities.

Cultivating Patience and Persistence Generating passive income requires patience and persistence. We'll explore the importance of adopting a long-term perspective and being patient with the process. We'll discuss techniques for staying motivated, persevering through challenges, and celebrating small wins along the way.

Embracing Failure as a Learning Opportunity Failure is an inevitable part of any journey, including the pursuit of passive income. We'll shift your perspective on failure and help you see it as a valuable learning opportunity rather than a setback. You'll discover how to bounce back from failure, extract lessons from it, and use those lessons to refine your strategies and grow stronger.

Developing a Growth Mindset A growth mindset is essential for your passive income journey. We'll explore the concept of a growth mindset, where you believe that your abilities and intelligence can be developed through dedication and hard work. You'll learn how to cultivate a growth mindset, embrace challenges, seek out feedback, and view setbacks as opportunities for growth and improvement.

Surrounding Yourself with Supportive Individuals The people you surround yourself with can greatly influence your success. We'll discuss the importance of building a supportive network of like-minded individuals who inspire and uplift you. You'll learn how to seek out mentors, join communities of passive income enthusiasts, and collaborate with others to accelerate your progress.

As you conclude this chapter on the mindset shift for passive income success, you now understand the importance of cultivating the right mindset for achieving your financial goals. By embracing an abundance mindset, overcoming limiting beliefs, cultivating patience and persistence, embracing failure as a learning opportunity, developing a growth mindset, and surrounding yourself with supportive individuals, you are primed for success on your passive income journey.

Remember, mindset is a powerful tool that can propel you forward or hold you back. As you continue on your path towards generating passive income, continue to nurture and strengthen your mindset. With the right mindset, you have the power to overcome obstacles, seize opportunities, and create the financial abundance and freedom you desire. Embrace this mindset shift, and watch as your passive income journey unfolds before your eyes.

INVESTING IN DIVIDEND STOCKS

Here we will explore the world of dividend stocks and how they can become a powerful tool in your passive income arsenal. Investing in dividend stocks allows you to generate a steady stream of passive income while benefiting from the potential growth of the stock market. Let's dive in and discover the benefits and strategies of investing in dividend stocks.

Understanding Dividend Stocks To begin, let's define what dividend stocks are and how they work. We'll explore how companies distribute a portion of their profits as dividends to shareholders. You'll learn the difference between dividend yield and dividend growth and how these factors play a role in selecting the right dividend stocks for your investment portfolio.

The Benefits of Dividend Stocks Investing in dividend stocks offers numerous advantages. We'll discuss these benefits, including:

- Steady Income: Dividend stocks provide a reliable source of passive income, allowing you to receive regular payments from your investments.

- Potential for Capital Appreciation: Dividend stocks can also offer the potential for capital appreciation, increasing the value of your investment over time.
- Diversification: Dividend stocks can help diversify your investment portfolio, reducing risk and providing stability.

Selecting Dividend-Paying Companies Choosing the right dividend-paying companies is crucial for successful dividend stock investing. We'll discuss factors to consider, such as company stability, historical dividend track record, and financial health. You'll learn how to research and evaluate companies to identify those that align with your investment goals.

Building a Diversified Dividend Portfolio Building a diversified dividend portfolio is essential to mitigate risk and maximize returns. We'll explore strategies for building a portfolio that spans different sectors and industries. You'll gain insights into asset allocation, risk management, and the importance of regularly reviewing and rebalancing your portfolio.

Reinvesting Dividends for Compounding Growth

One powerful aspect of dividend investing is the ability to reinvest dividends for compounding growth. We'll discuss the concept of dividend reinvestment plans (DRIPs) and how they can enhance the growth of your investment over time. You'll learn how reinvesting dividends can accelerate the growth of your passive income stream.

Managing Dividend Stock Investments Effective management of your dividend stock investments is essential for long-term success. We'll explore strategies for monitoring and evaluating your portfolio, including tracking dividend payments, analyzing company financials, and staying informed about market trends. You'll gain insights into when to buy, sell, or hold dividend stocks based on your investment goals.

As you conclude this chapter on investing in dividend stocks, you now have a solid understanding of how they can generate passive income and contribute to your financial goals. You've learned the benefits of dividend stocks, how to select dividend-paying companies, build a diversified portfolio, reinvest dividends for compounding growth, and effectively manage your investments.

Remember, investing in dividend stocks requires diligent research, patience, and a long-term perspective. It's essential to regularly review your portfolio, stay informed about market trends, and adjust your investment strategy as needed. By incorporating dividend stocks into your passive income journey, you can enjoy a reliable income stream while participating in the potential growth of the stock market.

RENTAL PROPERTY INVESTMENTS

Welcome to Chapter 4, where we'll explore the exciting world of rental property investments. Investing in rental properties can provide a reliable and consistent source of passive income. In this chapter, we'll delve into the benefits of rental property investments, the key considerations for success, and strategies for building a profitable rental property portfolio.

Understanding Rental Property Investments Let's begin by understanding the concept of rental property investments. We'll explore how purchasing and renting out properties can generate passive income. You'll learn about the different types of rental properties, including residential and commercial, and the potential benefits they offer.

- The Advantages of Rental Property Investments Investing in rental properties offers numerous advantages. We'll discuss these benefits, including:
- Regular Rental Income: Rental properties provide a consistent stream of passive income through monthly rental payments from tenants.

- Potential Appreciation: Properties have the potential to appreciate in value over time, increasing your overall wealth.

Tax Benefits: Rental property investments often come with tax advantages, such as deductions for mortgage interest, property taxes, and depreciation.

Section 3: Key Considerations for Rental Property Investments Successful rental property investments require careful consideration. We'll explore important factors to evaluate, including location, property condition, market demand, and rental regulations. You'll learn how to conduct market research and perform due diligence before making investment decisions.

Section 4: Financing Rental Property Investments Financing is a crucial aspect of rental property investments. We'll discuss different financing options, such as traditional mortgages, private lenders, or partnerships. You'll gain insights into loan requirements, down payments, and the importance of maintaining a healthy cash flow to cover expenses.

Section 5: Property Management and Tenant Relations Effectively managing rental properties and maintaining positive tenant relationships are essential for long-term success. We'll explore strategies for finding reliable property managers, setting rental rates, screening tenants, and handling maintenance and repairs. You'll learn how to foster positive tenant relations to ensure consistent rental income.

Section 6: Scaling Your Rental Property Portfolio Once you've established a successful rental property, you may desire to scale your portfolio. We'll discuss strategies for expanding your rental property investments, such as acquiring additional properties or diversifying across different locations. You'll gain insights into managing multiple properties and leveraging professionals to help streamline your operations.

Section 7: Mitigating Risks and Ensuring Profitability Investing in rental properties involves risks, and it's essential to mitigate them for long-term profitability. We'll explore strategies for reducing risk, such as having insurance coverage, conducting regular property inspections, and staying informed about market trends. You'll learn how to make informed decisions and adapt your investment strategy to maximize profitability.

Conclusion: As you conclude this chapter on rental

property investments, you now have a solid understanding of how they can generate passive income and contribute to your financial goals. You've learned about the benefits of rental property investments, key considerations for success, financing options, property management strategies, scaling your portfolio, and risk mitigation.

Remember, rental property investments require careful planning, ongoing management, and a commitment to providing quality housing for tenants. By incorporating rental properties into your passive income journey, you can build a profitable portfolio and enjoy the rewards of consistent rental income and potential property appreciation. So, let's continue on this exciting path, finding opportunities in the world of rental property investments and unlocking the potential for financial success.

BUILDING AN ONLINE BUSINESS

Welcome to Chapter 5, where we'll explore the world of building an online business as a means of generating passive income. In this chapter, we'll delve into the benefits of online entrepreneurship, the key considerations for success, and strategies for building a thriving online business.

Understanding Online Business Let's start by understanding what an online business entails. We'll explore how the internet has revolutionized the way we conduct business and how you can leverage online platforms to reach a global audience. You'll learn about different online business models and the potential benefits they offer.

The Advantages of an Online Business Building an online business offers numerous advantages. We'll discuss these benefits, including:

- Global Reach: With an online business, you can reach customers from around the world, expanding your market potential.
- Flexibility and Freedom: An online business allows you to work from anywhere, providing flexibility and the freedom to set your own schedule.

- Scalability: Online businesses have the potential to scale rapidly, reaching larger audiences and generating higher revenue.

Finding Your Online Business Idea A successful online business starts with a solid idea. We'll explore strategies for identifying a profitable niche and brainstorming business ideas that align with your interests, skills, and target market. You'll learn how to conduct market research, assess competition, and validate your business idea.

Setting Up Your Online Presence Establishing a strong online presence is crucial for the success of your online business. We'll discuss the key steps for setting up your website, creating engaging content, and optimizing it for search engines. You'll gain insights into selecting a domain name, choosing a website platform, and designing an appealing user experience.

Building Your Customer Base Attracting and building a loyal customer base is vital for the growth of your online business. We'll explore strategies for driving targeted traffic to your website, including search engine optimization (SEO), social media marketing, content marketing, and paid advertising. You'll learn how to engage with your audience, build trust, and convert visitors into customers.

Monetization Strategies for Your Online Business
Monetizing your online business is key to
generating passive income. We'll discuss different
monetization strategies, such as selling products or
services, affiliate marketing, advertising,
membership sites, or creating digital products.
You'll gain insights into selecting the right
monetization methods for your business and
maximizing your revenue potential.

Scaling and Outsourcing for Growth Once your
online business gains traction, you may desire to
scale and expand. We'll explore strategies for
scaling your operations, such as outsourcing tasks,
automating processes, or forming strategic
partnerships. You'll learn how to leverage
technology and professionals to help you grow
your business while maintaining a passive income
stream.

As you conclude this chapter on building an online
business, you now have a solid understanding of
how it can become a source of passive income and
contribute to your financial goals. You've learned
about the benefits of online entrepreneurship,
finding the right business idea, setting up your
online presence, building a customer base,

monetization strategies, and scaling for growth.

Remember, building a successful online business requires dedication, continuous learning, and adaptability to market trends. By embracing the opportunities provided by the digital landscape, you can create a thriving online business that generates passive income and provides you with the freedom and flexibility to live life on your own terms. So, let's dive into the world of online business and start building your path to financial independence.

CREATING AND SELLING DIGITAL PRODUCTS

Welcome to Chapter 6, where we'll explore the exciting realm of creating and selling digital products as a means of generating passive income. In this chapter, we'll delve into the benefits of digital products, the different types available, and strategies for successfully creating and selling them.

Understanding Digital Products Let's start by understanding what digital products are and how they can become a valuable source of passive income. We'll explore various types of digital products, including e-books, online courses, software, templates, and digital art. You'll learn how digital products can be easily created, replicated, and distributed to customers worldwide.

The Benefits of Digital Products Creating and selling digital products offers numerous advantages. We'll discuss these benefits, including:

- Digital products can be replicated and sold an unlimited number of times without incurring additional production costs.
- Low Overhead: With digital products, there

are no physical inventory or shipping costs, resulting in higher profit margins.

- Global Reach: Digital products can be accessed and purchased by customers from anywhere in the world, expanding your market potential.

Choosing Your Digital Product Selecting the right digital product is crucial for success. We'll discuss strategies for choosing a product that aligns with your expertise, target market, and income goals. You'll learn how to identify market demand, conduct research on competitors, and validate your product idea before investing time and effort.

Creating High-Quality Digital Content Creating high-quality digital content is essential to attract and engage customers. We'll explore techniques for developing compelling content that delivers value and solves specific problems for your target audience. You'll gain insights into content creation strategies, organizing your content effectively, and incorporating multimedia elements.

Platforms for Selling Digital Products Choosing the right platform to sell your digital products is crucial for reaching your target audience and managing transactions. We'll discuss popular platforms such as Gumroad, Teachable, Shopify, or Etsy, highlighting their features, pricing, and ease of use. You'll learn how to set up your digital storefront, optimize product listings, and leverage platform tools for marketing and sales.

Marketing and Promoting Your Digital Products Effective marketing is key to driving sales and generating passive income from your digital products. We'll explore strategies for marketing and promoting your products, including content marketing, email marketing, social media promotion, partnerships, and paid advertising. You'll gain insights into building your brand, engaging with your audience, and converting leads into customers.

Customer Support and Feedback Providing excellent customer support and gathering feedback is crucial for maintaining customer satisfaction and improving your digital products. We'll discuss strategies for offering prompt and helpful support, setting clear expectations, and actively seeking feedback from your customers. You'll learn how to leverage customer insights to refine and enhance your products.

As you conclude this chapter on creating and selling digital products, you now have a solid understanding of how they can become a valuable source of passive income. You've learned about the benefits of digital products, choosing the right product, creating high-quality content, selecting the appropriate platforms, marketing your products, and providing excellent customer support.

Remember, creating and selling digital products require a commitment to delivering value, ongoing marketing efforts, and a customer-centric approach. By leveraging your knowledge, skills, and creativity, you can create digital products that resonate with your target audience, generate passive income, and provide you with the freedom and flexibility to live life on your own terms. So, let's dive into the exciting world of digital product creation and start building your path to financial independence.

PEER-TO-PEER LENDING AND CROWDFUNDING

Welcome to Chapter 7, where we'll explore the fascinating opportunities presented by peer-to-peer lending and crowdfunding as avenues for generating passive income. In this chapter, we'll delve into the concepts of peer-to-peer lending and crowdfunding, their benefits, and strategies for maximizing returns through these platforms.

Understanding Peer-to-Peer Lending Let's begin by understanding the concept of peer-to-peer lending. We'll explore how peer-to-peer lending platforms connect borrowers and lenders directly, cutting out traditional financial institutions. You'll learn how to participate as a lender, earn interest on your loans, and diversify your investment portfolio through this alternative investment option.

The Benefits of Peer-to-Peer Lending Participating in peer-to-peer lending offers numerous advantages. We'll discuss these benefits, including:

- High Potential Returns: Peer-to-peer lending can provide higher returns compared to traditional savings accounts or bonds.
- Diversification: By lending to different borrowers, you can diversify your risk and potentially enhance your overall investment

portfolio.

- Passive Income: As a lender, you can earn passive income in the form of regular interest payments from borrowers.

Getting Started with Peer-to-Peer Lending To get started with peer-to-peer lending, you'll need to understand the process and choose a reputable lending platform. We'll discuss strategies for selecting the right platform, conducting due diligence on borrowers, and managing risk. You'll gain insights into setting investment criteria, diversifying your loans, and tracking your returns.

Exploring Crowdfunding Crowdfunding is another exciting avenue for generating passive income. We'll explore different types of crowdfunding, such as equity-based crowdfunding, donation-based crowdfunding, or reward-based crowdfunding. You'll learn how to leverage crowdfunding platforms to invest in or support projects, startups, or creative endeavors.

Benefits and Considerations of Crowdfunding Investing in crowdfunding projects offers unique benefits. We'll discuss these advantages, including:

- Early Access: Crowdfunding allows you to invest in innovative projects or support creative ideas before they reach the mainstream market.

- Potential for High Returns: Successful crowdfunding campaigns can yield significant returns if the project or startup experiences success.
- Supporting Causes and Innovations: Crowdfunding allows you to contribute to causes or projects that align with your values or interests.

Strategies for Successful Crowdfunding To maximize your returns and support meaningful projects through crowdfunding, we'll discuss strategies for successful participation. You'll learn how to evaluate crowdfunding campaigns, conduct research on the project or startup, and assess the credibility of the creators. We'll also explore the importance of diversifying your crowdfunding investments to manage risk.

Monitoring and Managing Your Peer-to-Peer Lending and Crowdfunding Investments To ensure the effectiveness of your peer-to-peer lending and crowdfunding investments, it's crucial to monitor and manage your portfolio. We'll explore strategies for tracking your loans, evaluating crowdfunding projects, and making informed decisions based on performance. You'll gain insights into adjusting your investments, reinvesting returns, and staying informed about industry trends.

As you conclude this chapter on peer-to-peer lending and crowdfunding, you now have a solid understanding of how these platforms can become valuable sources of passive income. You've learned about the benefits of peer-to-peer lending, getting started with lending platforms, exploring crowdfunding, and strategies for successful participation.

Remember, peer-to-peer lending and crowdfunding require thorough research, risk management, and ongoing monitoring of your investments. By participating in these alternative investment options, you can diversify your portfolio, earn passive income, and support innovative projects or causes. So, let's embrace the opportunities presented by peer-to-peer lending and crowdfunding, and open new doors to passive income generation.

HIGH-YIELD SAVINGS ACCOUNTS AND CDS

Welcome to Chapter 8, where we'll explore the reliable and low-risk options of high-yield savings accounts and certificates of deposit (CDs) as vehicles for generating passive income. In this chapter, we'll delve into the benefits of these financial instruments, their considerations, and strategies for maximizing returns while preserving capital.

Understanding High-Yield Savings Accounts Let's begin by understanding what high-yield savings accounts are and how they can help you generate passive income. We'll explore how these accounts offer higher interest rates compared to traditional savings accounts, allowing your money to grow over time. You'll learn about the advantages, accessibility, and safety features associated with high-yield savings accounts.

The Benefits of High-Yield Savings Accounts Investing in high-yield savings accounts offers several advantages. We'll discuss these benefits, including:

- Competitive Interest Rates: High-yield savings accounts provide higher interest rates than regular savings accounts, allowing your money to work harder for you.
- Liquidity: These accounts offer easy access to your funds when needed, providing flexibility and peace of mind.
- FDIC Insurance: High-yield savings accounts are typically insured by the Federal Deposit Insurance Corporation (FDIC), protecting your deposits up to a certain limit.

Selecting the Right High-Yield Savings Account To make the most of your investment, it's important to choose the right high-yield savings account. We'll discuss factors to consider, such as interest rates, fees, minimum balance requirements, and customer service. You'll gain insights into comparing different financial institutions and selecting an account that suits your needs and goals.

Understanding Certificates of Deposit (CDs) Certificates of Deposit (CDs) are another low-risk option for generating passive income. We'll explore how CDs work, where you deposit a fixed amount for a specific term at a predetermined interest rate.

You'll learn about the advantages, potential drawbacks, and different types of CDs available.

Evaluating CD Terms and Rates When investing in CDs, it's crucial to evaluate the terms and rates to maximize your returns. We'll discuss strategies for selecting CD terms that align with your investment goals and balancing them with liquidity needs. You'll gain insights into researching rates, understanding penalties for early withdrawal, and laddering your CD investments for a balanced approach.

Creating a Strategy with High-Yield Savings Accounts and CDs To optimize your passive income potential, it's essential to create a strategy that combines high-yield savings accounts and CDs. We'll explore strategies for allocating funds between these options based on your financial goals and risk tolerance. You'll gain insights into building a balanced portfolio that provides both liquidity and higher returns.

Managing Your High-Yield Savings Accounts and CDs Managing your high-yield savings accounts and CDs involves regular monitoring and decision-making. We'll discuss strategies for tracking interest rates, renewing or rolling over your CDs, and adjusting your investments as market conditions change. You'll learn how to make informed decisions to preserve capital, maximize returns, and ensure your passive income continues to grow.

As you conclude this chapter on high-yield savings accounts and CDs, you now have a solid understanding of how they can become valuable vehicles for generating passive income. You've learned about the benefits of high-yield savings accounts, selecting the right account, understanding CDs, evaluating terms and rates, creating a strategy, and managing your investments.

Remember, high-yield savings accounts and CDs offer stability, safety, and competitive returns for your passive income journey. By incorporating these low-risk options into your investment portfolio, you can enjoy the benefits of compounding interest, liquidity, and peace of mind. So, let's embrace the power of high-yield savings accounts and CDs, and watch as your passive income grows steadily over time.

ROYALTIES AND LICENSING

In this chapter, we'll explore the world of royalties and licensing as avenues for generating passive income. In this chapter, we'll delve into the concept of royalties and licensing, their benefits, and strategies for monetizing your creative works and intellectual property.

Understanding Royalties and Licensing Let's start by understanding what royalties and licensing entail. We'll explore how royalties are payments made to the owner of intellectual property, such as books, music, art, or inventions, in exchange for the use or sale of that property. You'll learn how licensing grants permission to others to use your intellectual property for a fee.

Benefits of Royalties and Licensing Generating income through royalties and licensing offers several advantages. We'll discuss these benefits, including:

- Passive Income Streams: Royalties and licensing provide a passive income stream as you earn income from the use of your intellectual property without active involvement.

- Expanding Reach: Licensing allows your work to reach a wider audience through collaborations with other businesses or individuals.
- Asset Value: Intellectual property with royalty or licensing potential holds value, which can appreciate over time and provide long-term income.

Monetizing Your Creative Works If you're a creative individual, you can monetize your works through royalties and licensing. We'll explore strategies for protecting your creative works through copyrights, trademarks, or patents. You'll learn how to leverage platforms, such as publishing houses, music labels, or licensing agencies, to monetize your creations and negotiate fair agreements.

Navigating the Licensing Process Licensing your intellectual property requires careful consideration and negotiation. We'll discuss strategies for identifying potential licensing opportunities, conducting market research, and evaluating licensing agreements. You'll gain insights into setting licensing terms, protecting your rights, and leveraging legal assistance when necessary.

Maximizing Royalty Income Maximizing your royalty income requires proactive management of your intellectual property. We'll explore strategies for royalty collection, tracking usage, and enforcing rights. You'll learn how to effectively manage contracts, audit royalty statements, and explore new opportunities for licensing or distribution.

Expanding into New Markets and Formats To maximize your royalty and licensing potential, it's important to explore new markets and formats for your intellectual property. We'll discuss strategies for adapting your works into different formats, such as eBooks, audiobooks, merchandise, or adaptations for film or television. You'll gain insights into collaborating with professionals and leveraging their expertise to expand your reach.

Protecting Your Intellectual Property Protecting your intellectual property is essential to safeguard your rights and maximize your passive income potential. We'll explore strategies for copyright registration, trademark protection, and patent applications. You'll learn how to enforce your rights, address infringement, and work with legal professionals to ensure the integrity of your intellectual property.

As you conclude this chapter on royalties and

licensing, you now have a solid understanding of how they can become valuable sources of passive income. You've learned about the benefits of royalties and licensing, monetizing your creative works, navigating the licensing process, maximizing income, expanding into new markets, and protecting your intellectual property.

Remember, royalties and licensing provide an opportunity to generate income from your creative works and intellectual property long after their creation. By effectively managing your intellectual property, negotiating fair agreements, and exploring new opportunities, you can enjoy the benefits of passive income while protecting your creative rights. So, let's embrace the potential of royalties and licensing, and watch as your intellectual property generates passive income and adds value to your financial journey.

CREATING MULTIPLE STREAMS OF PASSIVE INCOME

Welcome to the final chapter of our journey towards passive income success. In this chapter, we'll explore the power of creating multiple streams of passive income to enhance your financial security and freedom. We'll discuss the benefits, strategies, and considerations for diversifying your income sources and building a resilient passive income portfolio.

The Power of Multiple Streams of Passive Income Creating multiple streams of passive income offers numerous advantages. We'll discuss these benefits, including:

- Income Stability: Diversifying your income sources reduces dependence on a single stream, providing stability and protection against potential fluctuations.
- Increased Income Potential: Multiple streams of passive income allow you to earn from various sources, potentially increasing your overall earning potential.
- Risk Mitigation: Spreading your investments across different income streams helps

manage risk and minimizes the impact of a single income source underperforming.

Identifying Additional Passive Income Opportunities To create multiple streams of passive income, you need to identify additional opportunities. We'll discuss strategies for exploring new income sources, such as real estate investments, dividend stocks, online businesses, peer-to-peer lending, digital products, and more. You'll learn how to assess each opportunity's potential and align them with your goals and interests.

Evaluating Risk and Return on Investment As you consider additional passive income opportunities, it's important to evaluate the associated risks and potential returns. We'll discuss risk assessment techniques, diversification strategies, and methods for analyzing the return on investment (ROI) for each income stream. You'll gain insights into balancing high-risk, high-reward investments with more stable and predictable options.

Developing a Diversified Passive Income Portfolio Building a diversified passive income portfolio requires careful planning and implementation. We'll explore strategies for allocating your resources across different income streams, considering factors such as risk tolerance, time commitment, and investment requirements. You'll learn how to create a portfolio that balances short-term income with long-term growth potential.

Managing and Monitoring Your Portfolio Effectively managing and monitoring your passive income portfolio is crucial for sustained success. We'll discuss strategies for tracking income, assessing performance, and making informed decisions. You'll gain insights into setting financial goals, regularly reviewing your portfolio, and adjusting your strategies based on changing market conditions.

Continual Learning and Adaptation To thrive in the world of passive income, continual learning and adaptation are essential. We'll explore the importance of staying informed about industry trends, exploring new opportunities, and expanding your knowledge. You'll learn how to adapt your strategies and embrace emerging income streams to stay ahead of the curve.

Embracing Financial Freedom Creating multiple streams of passive income brings you closer to achieving financial freedom. We'll discuss the concept of financial freedom and how passive income can provide the flexibility to live life on your own terms. You'll gain insights into setting meaningful financial goals, creating a plan for achieving them, and celebrating milestones along the way.

In conclusion, this final chapter on creating multiple streams of passive income, you now have a comprehensive understanding of the power and potential of diversifying your income sources. You've learned the benefits of multiple streams, identified additional passive income opportunities, evaluated risk and return on investment, developed a diversified portfolio, and embraced the principles of continual learning and adaptation.Remember, creating multiple streams of passive income requires careful planning, risk management, and ongoing monitoring. By diversifying your income sources, you can build a resilient portfolio that generates income from various streams and provides financial security and freedom. So, let's take action, embrace the opportunities presented by passive income, and embark on a journey that leads to a life of abundance and fulfillment.